DISCOVER
Undersea Malta

by
Mark Gisler
Illustrated by Jeni Caruana

PEG
PUBLICATIONS

For Miko and Sibby,
who inspire me to be better than I am

Publishers Enterprises Group (PEG) Ltd
P.E.G. Building, UB7 Industrial Estate,
San Gwann SGN 09, Malta

Web Site: http://www.peg.com.mt
E.mail: contact@peg.com.mt

First published 2000

ISBN: 99909-0-262-3

Printed in Malta by P.E.G. Ltd, San Gwann

On the
beautiful Isle of
Malta another
sunny day is dawning.
Malta is actually a group of three islands –
Malta, Gozo and Comino – in the middle of the Mediterranean.
Malta is 100 kilometers (62 miles) from Italy (in either
kilometers or miles, that's much too far for anyone to swim).

In Manikata, the Manduca family is still asleep.
Inside their house . . .

meet Marisa. She is six years old. The tooth fairy has visited
her twice. Marisa is a Girl Scout. She loves dolphins, dinosaurs
and pizza. Marisa also enjoys reading and has a puppy named
Newt. Next door to her room . . .

4

is Marisa's brother Stefan. He has just turned ten and wants to be a pilot when he grows up. He loves to play football, skateboard and is learning to play the guitar (his parents are glad that he has given up the drums). He also enjoys swimming.
Across the hall . . .

their parents are already awake. Marisa's father is a professor of marine biology and oceanography (the study of the sea and its creatures). He knows more than anyone about the sea life of Malta (this comes in handy since Marisa and Stefan ask so many questions). Marisa's mother is an artist. Her favourite subject (besides Marisa and Stefan) is the sea. She also makes the best *timpana* in Malta. The whole family is about to have a very BIG DAY!

"Wake up Marisa, I have a surprise for you!" Her father hands her a package containing a mask, fins and snorkel. "Put on your swimsuit. You are going snorkeling at Għar Lapsi with your brother and me this morning. I know you will love the amazing sea creatures and plants that live in the beautiful waters of Malta." Marisa shoots straight out of bed and grabs her swimsuit and towel. "Yahoo!" she exclaims. "I'm finally going snorkeling!"

Marisa can hardly contain her excitement. She quickly tries on her mask (it smells like new plastic). Her father had been taking Stefan snorkeling with him for more than a year now. Every time they returned, she listened to their stories of their adventures and descriptions of the creatures they saw under the sea. Her father had promised to take her with them as soon as she passed her advanced swimming class. Yesterday she passed! Now she will finally join them!

Make sure your mask fits securely to your face and the snorkel is positioned so that it sticks up when your face is in the water" her father explains. "Also, it's easier to put on your equipment if it's already wet." Marisa had listened carefully to these instructions when Stefan was learning. She had also tried on all of Stefan's equipment many times when he was not looking. "I know Dad! Let's go!" Marisa's mother observes the lesson and smiles at her daughter's excitement.

"The sea can be a very dangerous place if you are not prepared or are not paying close attention" her father cautions. "You must stay close by me. I will identify the plants and creatures we see. Some of them have sharp spines or stingers. You must not touch anything until you know it's safe." Marisa listens carefully. "We should keep in mind that when we visit the undersea environment we are guests in someone else's home. We may look at the plants and animals and even touch some of them. But we must always avoid harming them or their homes" explains Marisa's father. Marisa nods her head in understanding.

As soon as they leave the shore, Marisa finds that she is entering a totally new world. It seems so quiet. The water tastes very salty. Marisa is just getting used to the strange sensation of breathing through her snorkel when suddenly . . .

as if to greet them, three Bottlenosed Dolphins approach them. Dolphins are mammals, not fish, who must surface to breathe, but can stay underwater for as long as one hour. They are also Marisa's favourite kind of animal. She waves at them and they seem to smile back at her.

As they pass by a large rock, Marisa's father points out a bright red Common Starfish. Although the starfish might appear to be a plant because it moves so slowly, it is actually an animal. In fact, if Marisa were patient enough to watch this starfish all day long, she could see it attack and capture its food in super-slow motion (making the starfish one of the world's slowest predators).

They swim near a small cave and Stefan discovers two Parrotfish. He knows that the female of the species is more vividly coloured than the male (Parrotfish are named for their bright colours, not because they squawk). These Parrotfish hardly notice Stefan because they are so busy eating algae from the wall of the cave.

Near a crevice in the rocks,
the three divers see an Octopus.
The Octopus is often very hard to see
since it can change colour to match
its environment. It also is able to
squirt black ink when threatened.
Wary of the visitors, the Octopus
swims quickly away by forcing water
through a tube in its body, creating a
powerful jet.

14

Just then, a school of Greater Amberjack comes into view, moving as if it were one creature. These fish can grow to be nearly two meters long, are very fast swimmers and are generally found in large schools in open water. The snorkelers turn to follow, but the Amberjack school is moving much too quickly.

Closer to shore, Marisa's father gestures toward some Rock Urchins. Although they look like spiny plants, urchins are animals too. They use their spines to move across the rocks. Rock Urchins are very common near the rocky shores in many parts of Malta and Gozo. As a result, they are known to cause Maltese swimmers to tread lightly!

Near its home in a cave, a large Dusky Grouper watches them. It is the biggest fish Marisa has ever seen. Although they are still common, the number of Groupers has decreased in recent years. Groupers are solitary fish who prefer not to attend "schools". One enormous Grouper who lives in the Blue Hole near Gozo's Azur Window has been nicknamed "King Arthur" by local divers.

Nearby, they see a cluster of Dog Worms. These Worms (also known as Fire Worms) have tiny bristles on each segment of their bodies that serve as "feet" to grip and move about. The white tufts of bristles along the sides of their bodies contain venom and can inflict a nasty sting if touched. "A Dog Worm's bite is worse than its bark," Marisa's father warns.

As they move into deeper water they see a Loggerhead Turtle swim beneath them. Marisa knows that they are very lucky because the Loggerhead is a very rare sight in Malta these days. Before the 1930's, large numbers of these turtles used to lay their eggs in the warm sandy beach of Ramla l-Ħamra in Gozo. Now these magnificent turtles have been hunted for their meat, eggs and shells to the brink of extinction.

They all dive down near the bottom. Partially hidden in the sea grass, they see a Red Scorpionfish. It is very shy and retreats into the rocks. Marisa knows that the dorsal fin spines of the Red Scorpionfish are poisonous, so she keeps a respectful distance.

Nearby is a Greater Angler Fish, a rather unusual predator. The Angler Fish hides buried in the sand and extends a "lure" on the first spine of its dorsal fin to attract prey. It is the first time that any of them have seen a fish "fish."

Next they see three Shore Hermit Crabs. Hermit Crabs live in empty snail shells. They feed on tiny bits of food and other organic material that fall to the bottom. Thus, Hermit Crabs can rightly be called the "garbage men" of the sea.

A school of Flying Fish cruises by and suddenly leaps out of the water near them. Usually as a means of escape, the Flying Fish is able to "fly" for short distances by jumping out of the water and using its two extra-large fins to glide through the air.

They swim down to see two Patched Dorids creeping along the surface of a sponge. They are members of the mollusk family and are close cousins of snails. Patched Dorids rely on one particular species of sponge as their sole source of food.

Stefan inspects a school of Short-nosed Seahorses. Stefan identifies the father Seahorses because he knows that the eggs laid by the females are carried in pouches in the bellies of the males. These are some of the only fathers in the world who know what it's like to be pregnant.

Below them in the sand, Marisa's father points out a Common Stingray. The end of the Stingray's spine protrudes from its tail and forms a stinger that can cause serious wounds to swimmers. The Stingray likes to bury itself on the sandy bottom to wait for unsuspecting prey.

They find themselves in a shimmering school of Saddled Bream. Each Bream seems to know exactly when the school plans to change direction, so the school seems to move as one gigantic fish. Bream typically feed on algae and are one of the most abundant fish in Malta.

Just before they return to shore,
the divers marvel at a bright orange colony of Golden Zoanthids.
While they look like flowers, when Stefan views them close up
he can see that they actually are small animals similar to
Anemone. The Golden Zoanthids wave gently in the current
almost as if to say "thanks for visiting, come back soon."

28

Marisa, Stefan and their father leave the water dripping and talking excitedly about the things they have seen. Marisa's mother shows them her just-finished drawing of the small island of Filfla. Marisa feels privileged to have been invited into the undersea home of so many amazing creatures. Stefan exclaims "didn't I tell you how great it was!"

29

Can you help Marisa identify all the creatures she saw?

Bottle-nosed Dolphin *(Tursiops truncatus) Denfil Geddumu Qasir*

Common Starfish *(Echinaster sepositus) Stilla Ħamra*

Parrotfish *(Sparisoma cretense) Mrażpan*

Octopus *(Octopus vulgaris) Qarnita*

Greater Amberjack *(Seriola dumerili) Aċċola*

Rock Urchin *(Paracentrotus lividus) Rizza*

Dusky Grouper *(Epinephelus gauza) Ċerna*

Dog (or Fire) Worm *(Herodice carunculata) Busuf*

Loggerhead Turtle *(Caretta caretta) Fekruna Komuni*

Red Scorpionfish *(Scorpaena scrofa) Ċippulazza*

Greater Angler Fish *(Lophius piscatorius) Petriċa Kbira*

Shore Hermit Crabs *(Cibanarius erythropus) Granċ*

Flying Fish *(Cheilopogon heterus) Rondinella Komuni*

Patched Dorids *(Discodoris atromaculata) Serduq tat-Tbajja'*

Short-nosed Seahorses *(Hippocampus hippocampus) Żiemel tal-Baħar Ħalqu Qasir*

Common Stingray *(Dasyatis pastinaca) Boll Komuni*

Saddled Bream *(Oblada melanura) Kaħlija*

Golden Zoanthids *(Parazoanthus axinellae) Artikla Safra*

As they drove away, Marisa's father said "I hope you enjoyed your first view under the waters of Malta. Next time we'll go snorkeling in Gozo." But Marisa could not answer him. With all the excitement of the day, she had fallen asleep and was dreaming of their next adventure.